Pixels

DIEGo Joe

Barrio Quintero

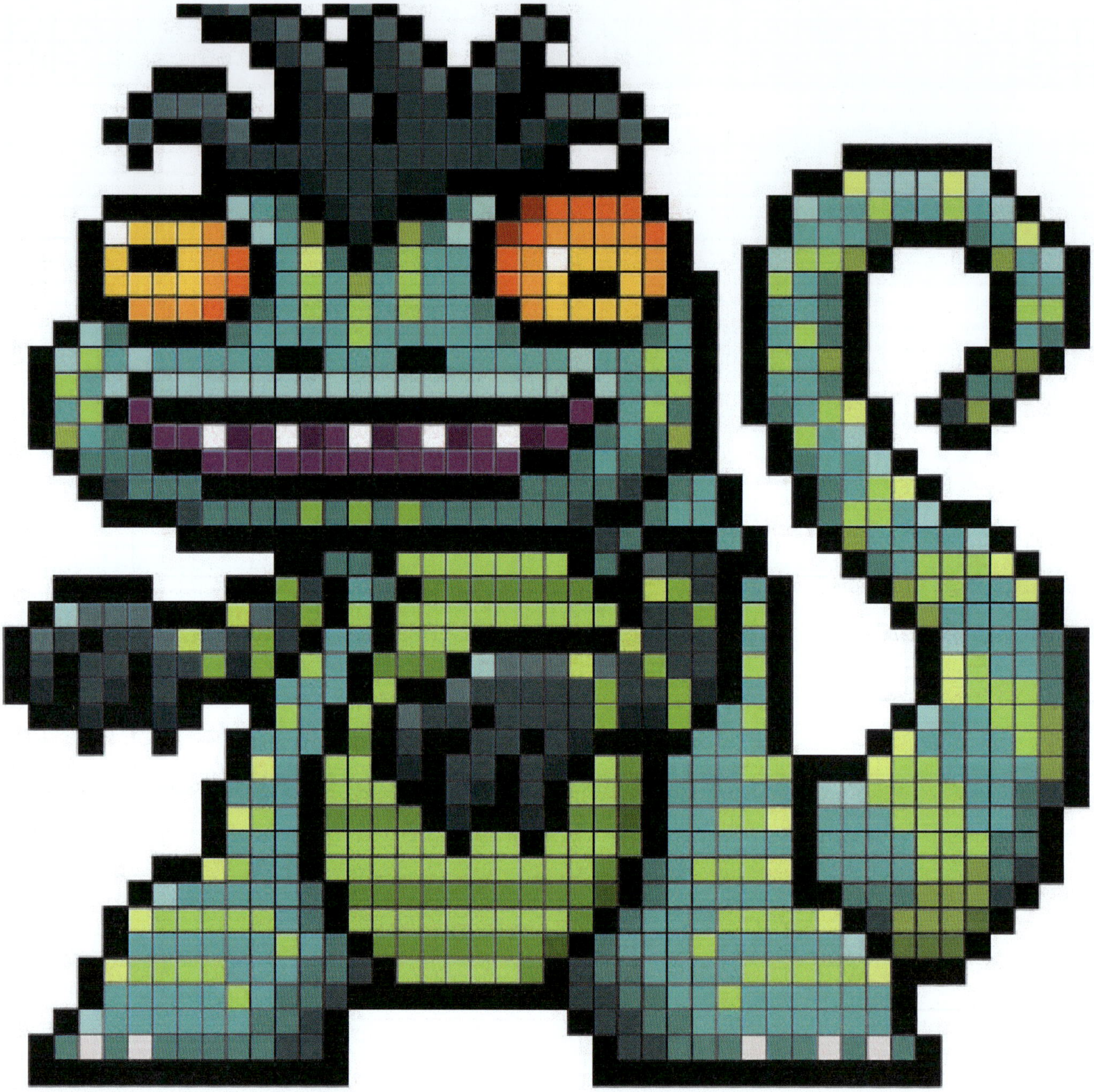

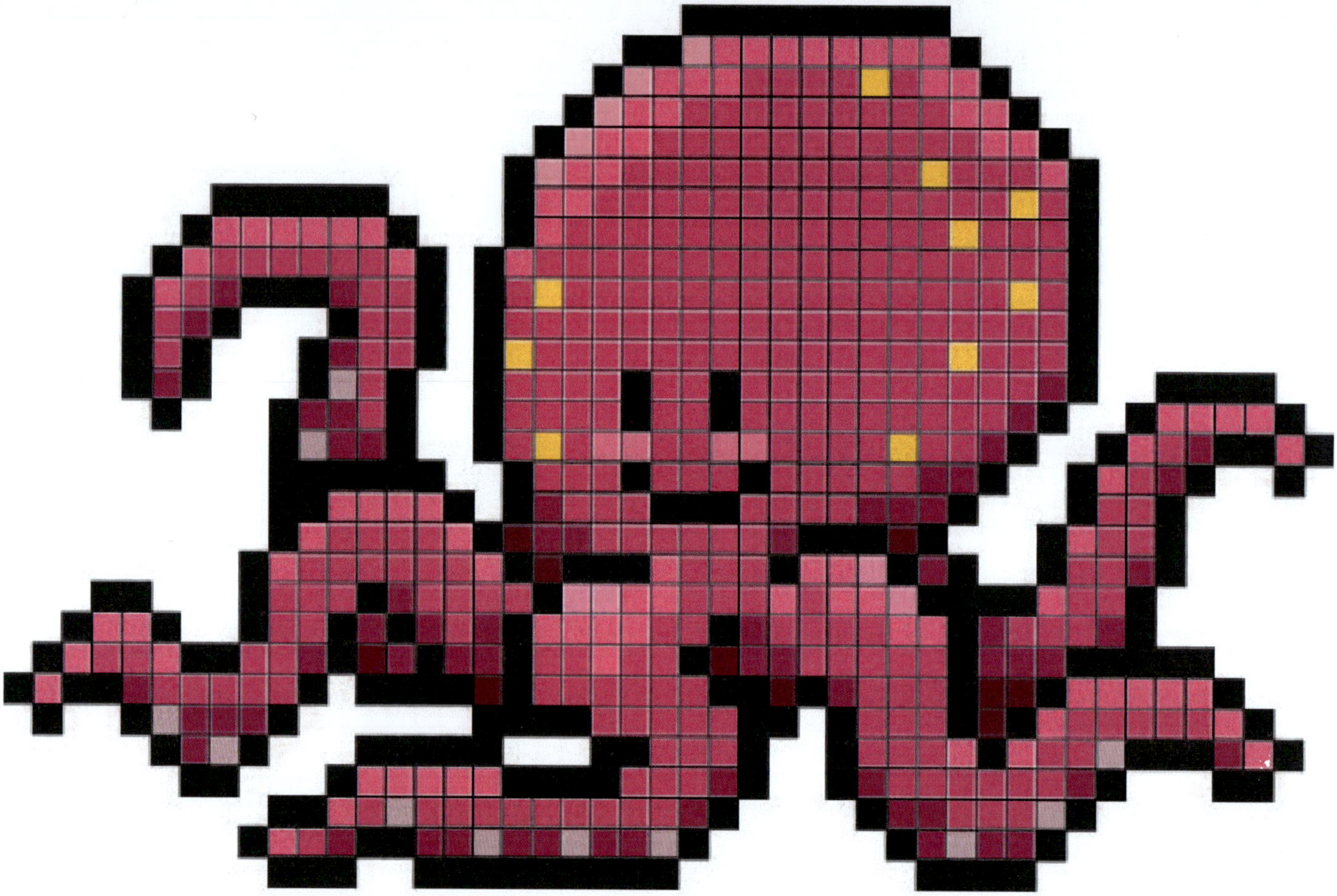

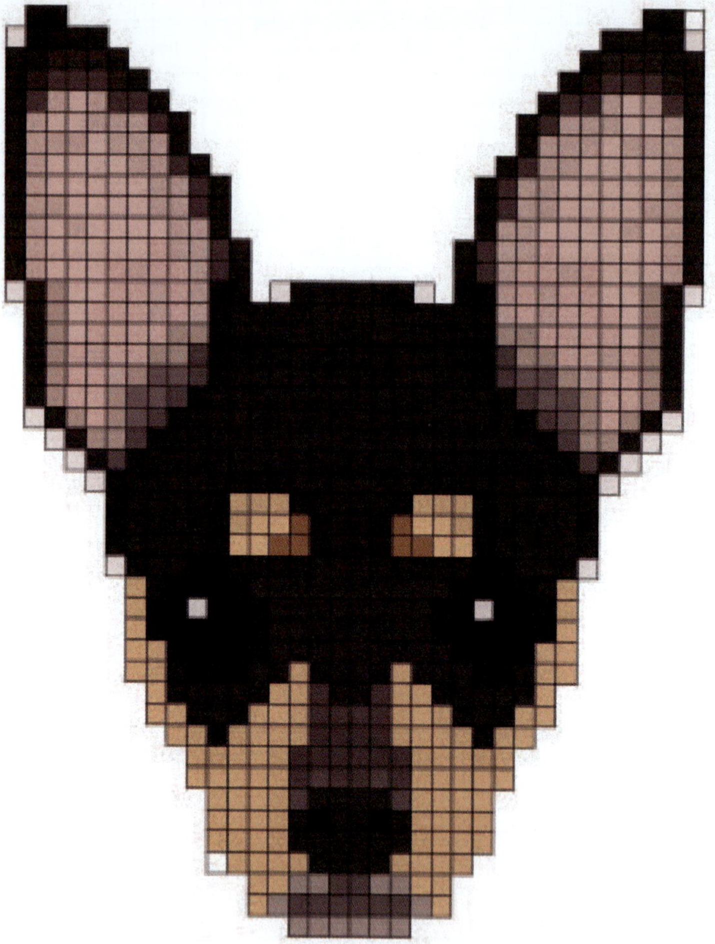

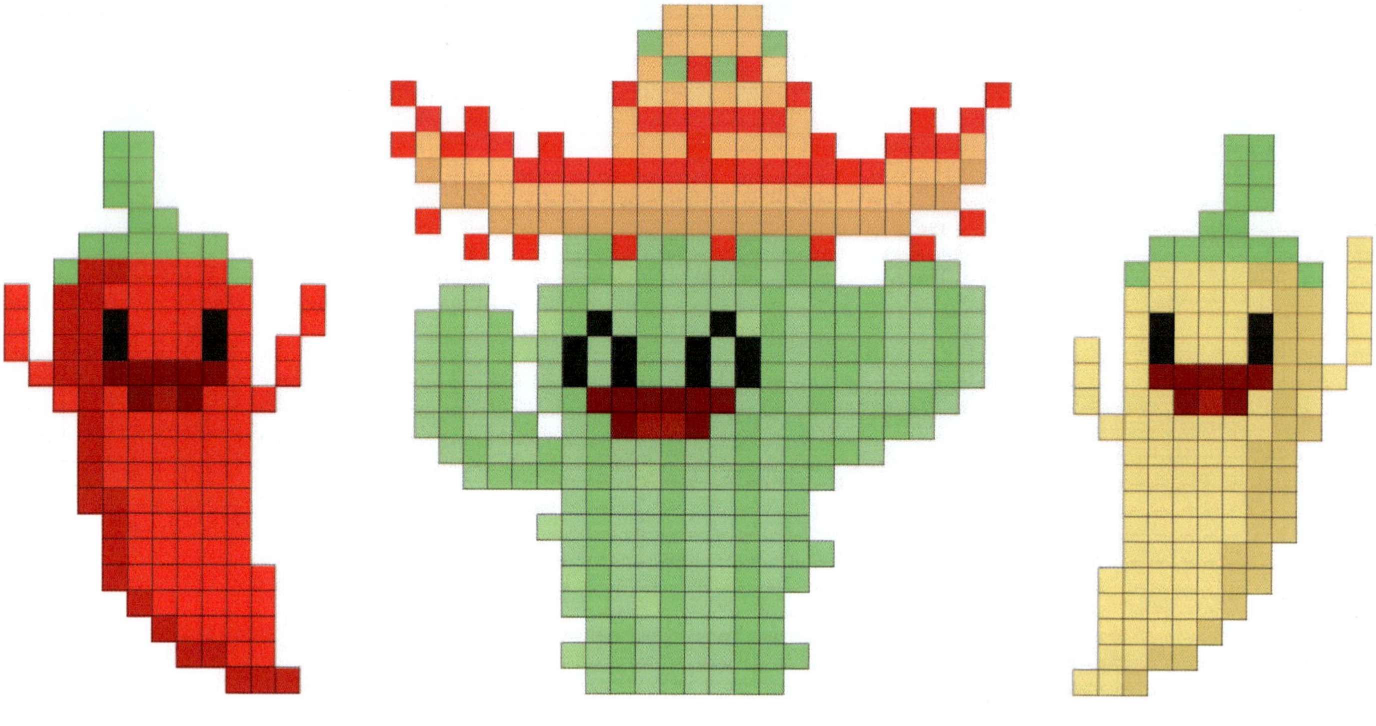

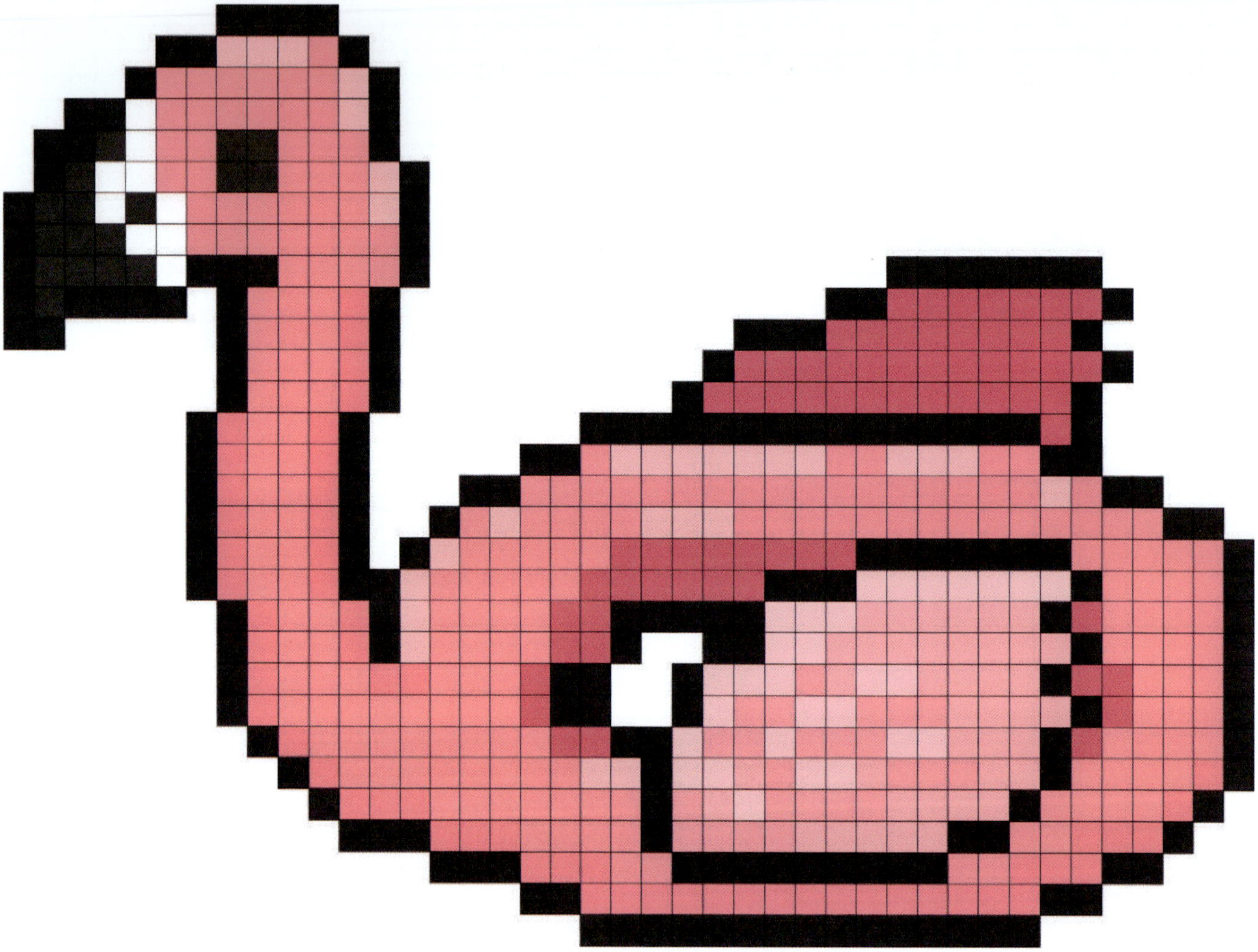

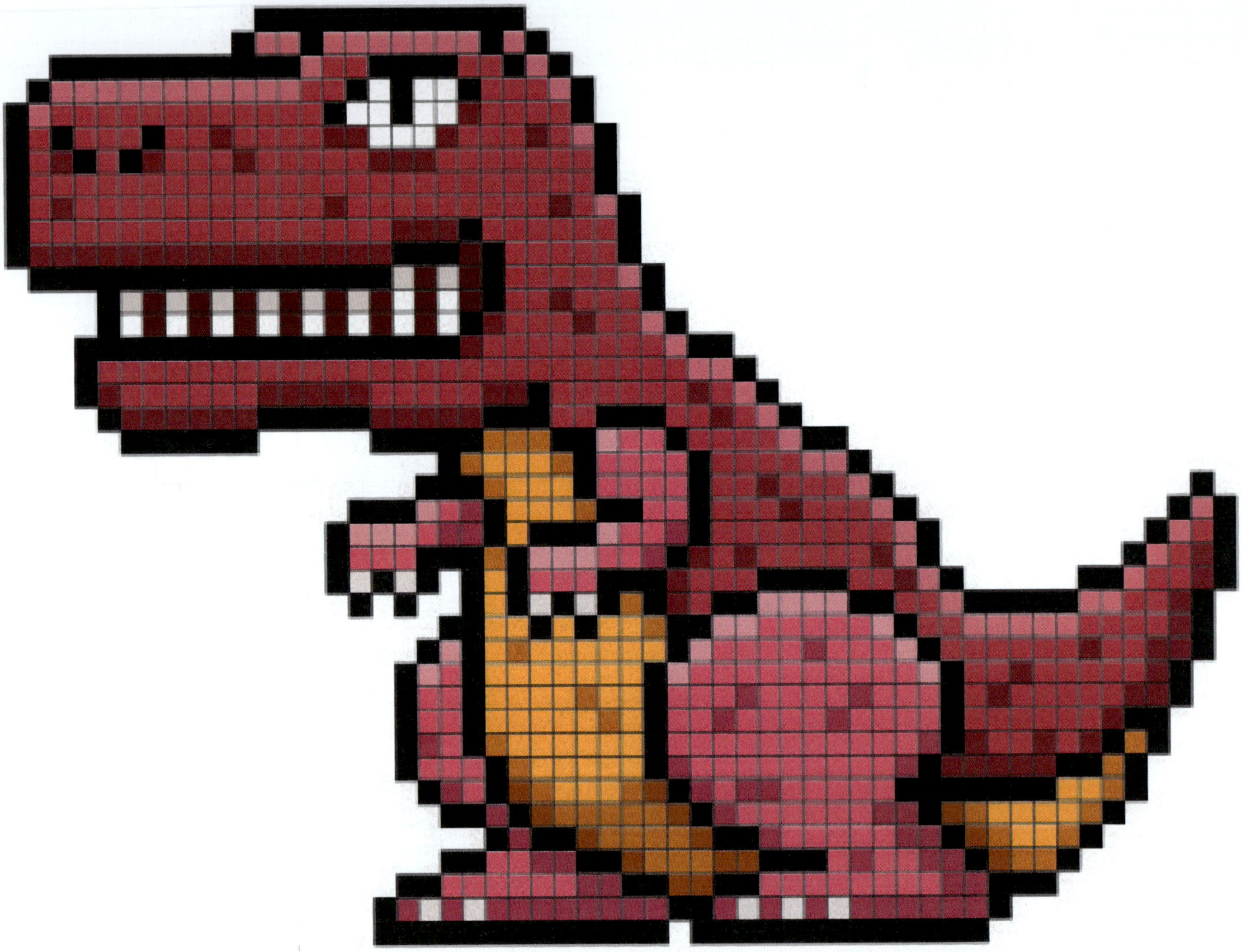

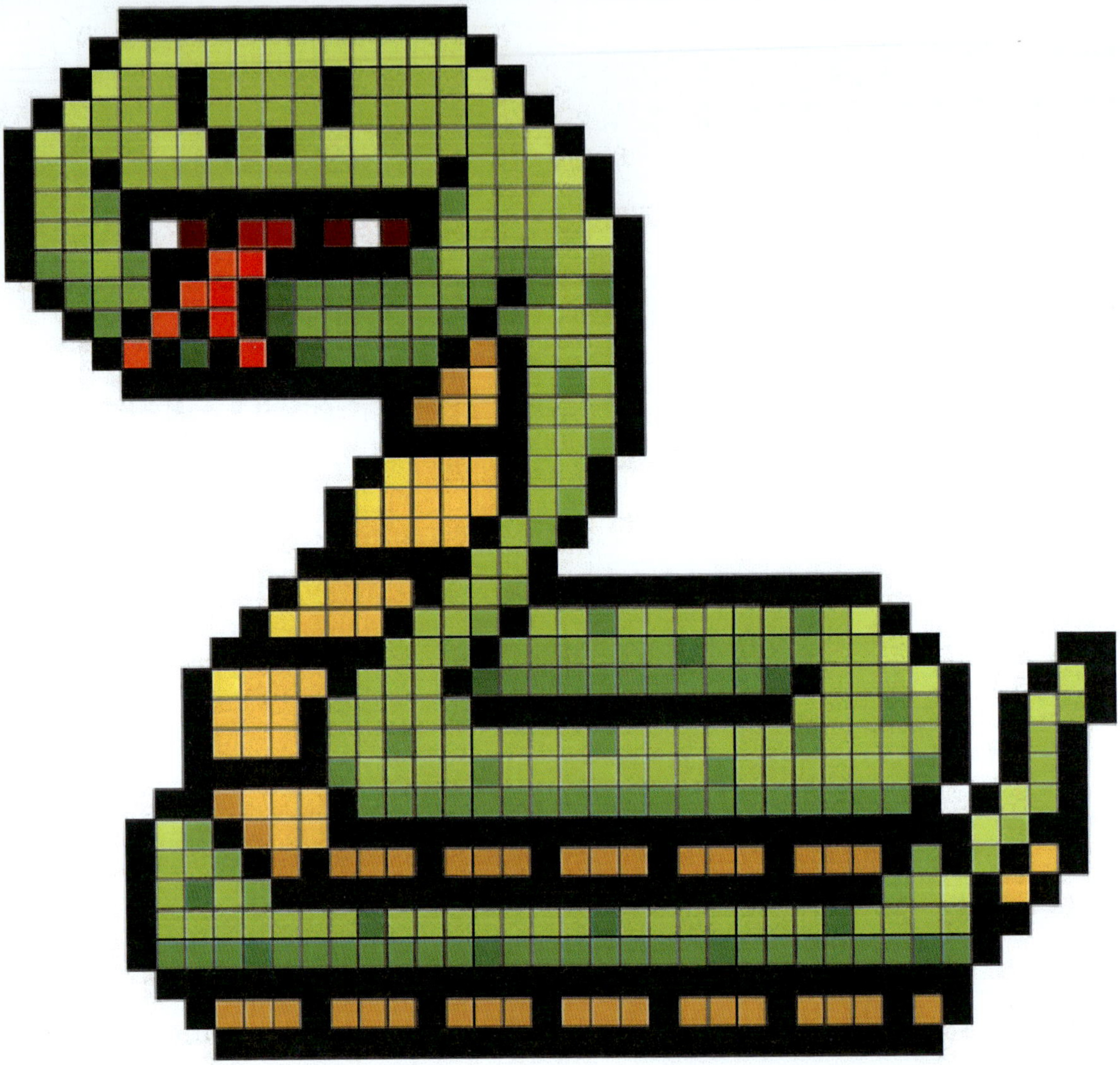

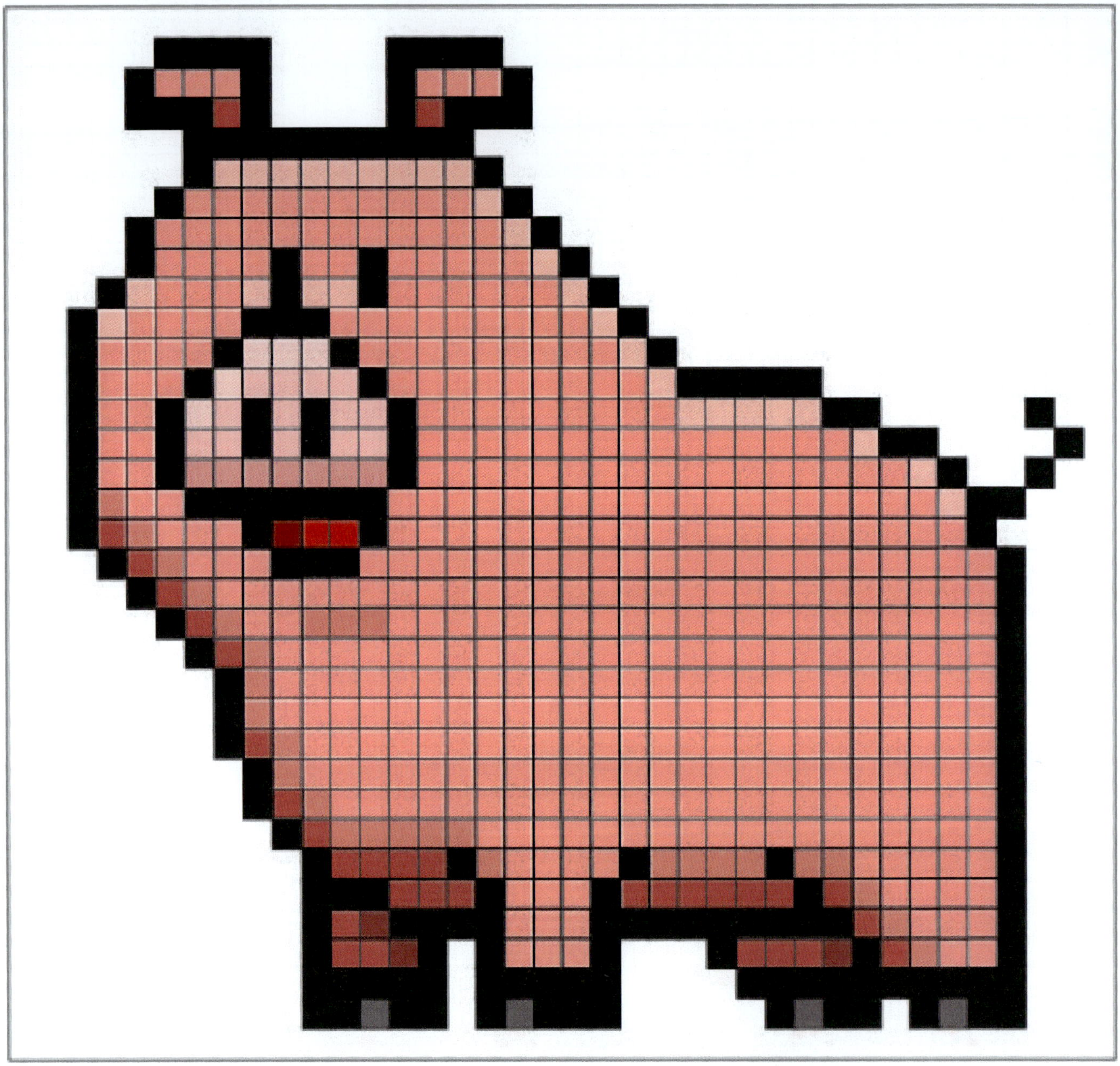

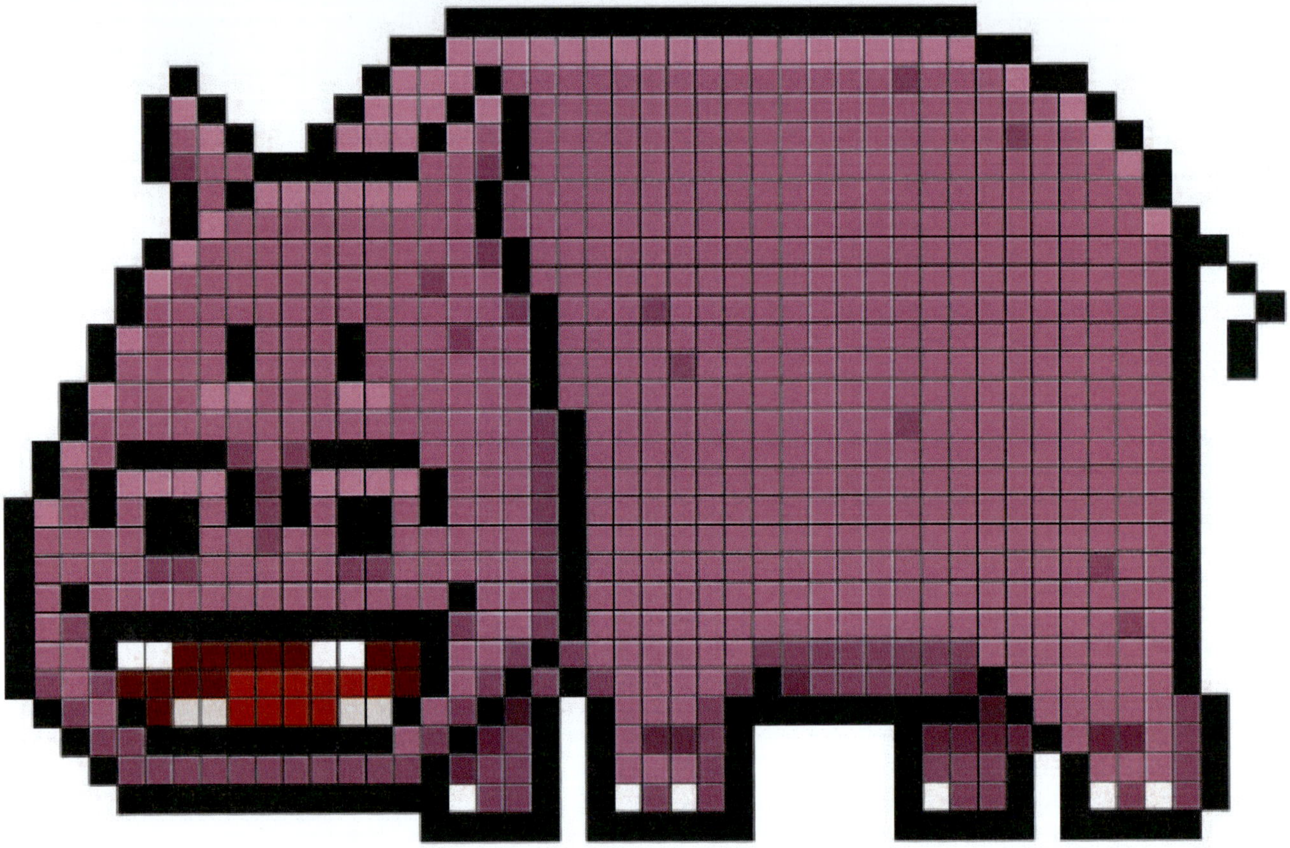

POLICE

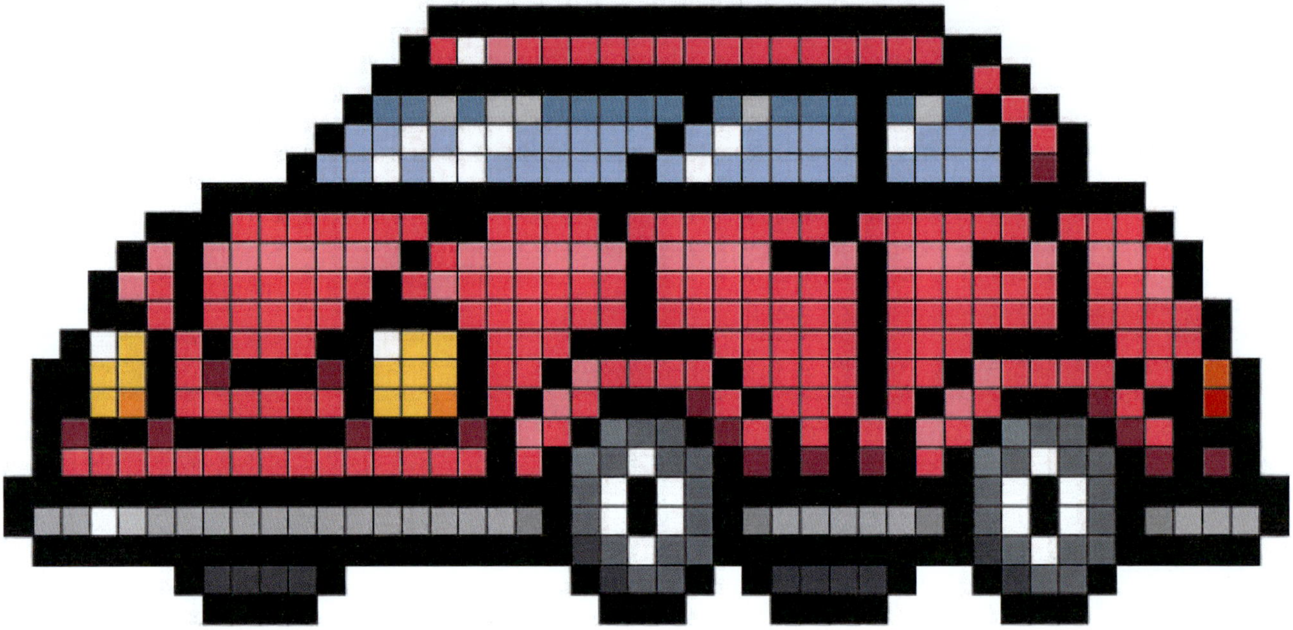

Printed by Amazon Italia Logistica S.r.l.
Torrazza Piemonte (TO), Italy

27500142R00025